*Dedicated to friends
who come & friends who go...
wherever the winds
may take us, fond memories
of times shared will
forever remain.*

About FRIENDSHIP

Thoughts, Hopes, Reflections

WRITTEN & ILLUSTRATED BY

Lynne Gerard

the C.R. Gibson Company
Norwalk, Connecticut 06856

There is something
exceptional about
friendship which is
life-giving to the
soul.

The people we meet,
especially the
friends we keep,
are sent to us...
and we are sent to them,
for the mutual
purpose of
support and
discovery.

This means that
our friendship is not a
chance occurrence...

...our paths have crossed for a special reason.

You and I have been given the opportunity to consider life through each other's personal perceptions.

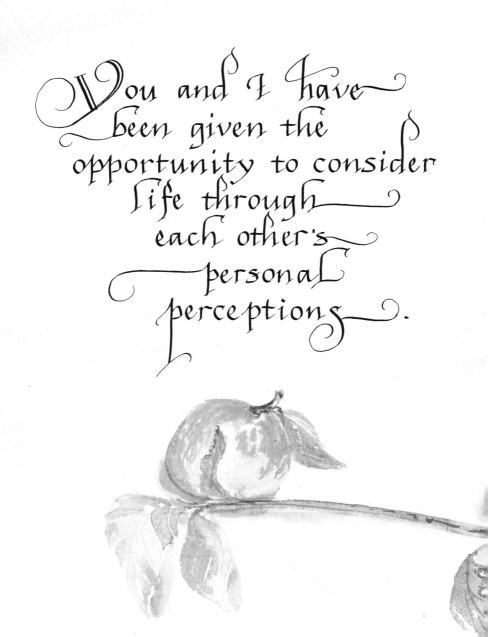

I take notice
of things you feel
are important...

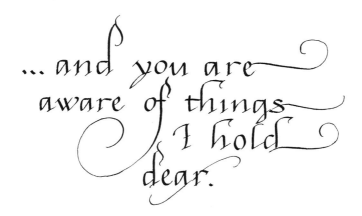

...and you are
aware of things
I hold
dear.

Friendship helps
us develop greater
sensitivity
and empathy,

Lynne
Gerard

as we learn
to respect a
different point
of view.

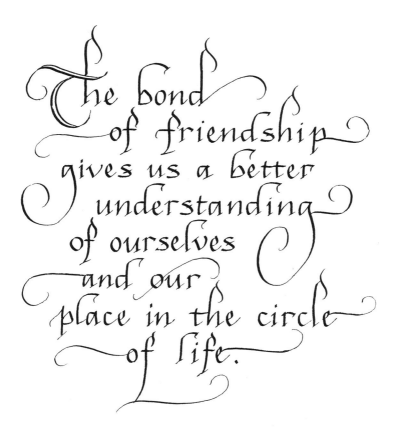

The bond
of friendship
gives us a better
understanding
of ourselves
and our
place in the circle
of life.

Each of us
is an
important
part of all
that
is.

You are unique,
and I am unique...

...each of us possess
special God-given
apptitudes.

Through
friendship we
help each other
recognize and develop
our inner
potentials.

We share
each other's
sorrows and
joys.

We uplift
each other
when apprehension
tries to
overwhelm
hope.

We give each other
the courage
to use the
strength within
to persevere
and triumph.

Lynne Gerard

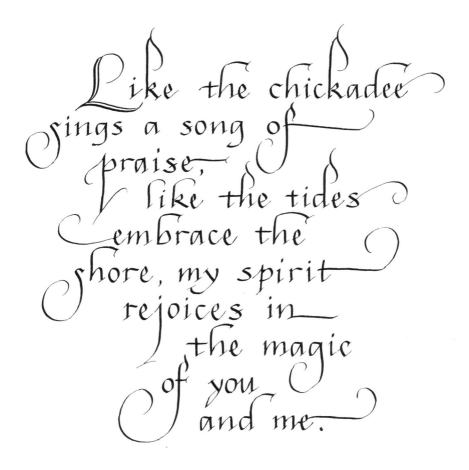

Like the chickadee
sings a song of
praise,
like the tides
embrace the
shore, my spirit
rejoices in
the magic
of you
and me.

Life is much more than what it seems, and much more than what we know...

...for each day is a
new discovery, and we
cannot say what tomorrow's
wind may bring.

Yet, of this I
am certain;
knowing you has
made me a
better person,

and I will
forever hold a
part of
you
within me.

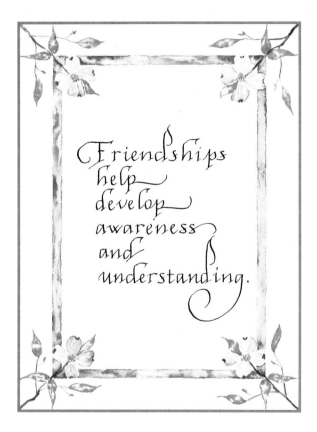

Friendships
help
develop
awareness
and
understanding.